Adventure in Education

Resources in Education

Other titles in this Series:

Resources in Education

Adventure in Education

Team building through outdoor pursuits

Richard Andrews

Northcote House

First published in 1997 by Northcote House Publishers Ltd, Plymbridge House, Estover Road, Plymouth PL6 7PY, United Kingdom.
Tel: +44 (0) 1752 202368. Fax: +44 (0) 1752 202330.

British Library Cataloguing-in-Publication Data
A catalogue record for this book is available from the British Library.

ISBN 0-7463-0682 2

Typeset by PDQ Typesetting, Newcastle-under-Lyme
Printed and bound by in the United Kingdom

This book is dedicated to
Chief and Unai
who both had so much to offer

What we have to learn to do we learn by doing – Aristotle

Contents

Acknowledgements

Team Dynamics – for the inspiration.

Oliver Carpenter – for a lesson in computers.

The Children of St. Anselm's School – for their willing participation and eager enthusiasm.

The Physical Education Department of St. Anselm's School – for their help and support towards implementation of the adventure programme.

Anja Bradley – with her computer, for helping me wade through all the paperwork.

Charlotte Firmin – for her captivating illustrations.

Foreword

Jennifer Newman

Jennifer Newman monitors, advises and supports primary, secondary and special schools in Kent in all aspects of physical education. This includes outdoor and adventurous activities. She also is an OFSTED inspector of schools. Her own interests are white water canoeing, skiing and mountaineering.

There is a great need for a better understanding of adventure within our school society: 'a state of mind that begins with uncertainty... and results in a feeling of elation'; the definition of teams as being something more than the wrongly perceived sporting definition – leadership opportunities for all, not only for the elite. A broad understanding is often absent, not only amongst the school population at large but also amongst physical education teachers. *Adventure in Education* sets out to provide many elements necessary for such an understanding and at the same time is a refreshingly realistic read. It seeks to educate the teacher about adventure within the curriculum, and provides many appropriate and accessible ideas to use with pupils. It is not a compilation of ideas taken from a detached, objective position, but engages the reader with the reality of class and school. From the outset the major premise is that adventure in education is an exciting discipline which should be made fully accessible to all young people and which prepares them for society.

The need for a book of this type is borne out by teachers grasping at less comprehensive volumes with desperation. In our educational system the majority of schools do not offer outdoor and adventurous activities as a subject after the primary level and many primary schools are struggling to implement a worthwhile programme. Richard Andrews confirms the value of participating in an education which provides opportunities to solve problems, interact with peers, build self-confidence, work within a team, establish self-esteem, make decisions, be reflective and be critically analytical.

Readers are urged to read the book from cover to cover so that the whole spectrum of adventure in education is uncovered. The obvious commitment and enthusiasm which the author reflects in his book carries the reader through the 'dictates' of the National Curriculum into the inspiring realm of realistic examples of activities which can be undertaken within the school grounds. Each teacher will be heartened by what can be done inside the current curriculum restraints and structures.

To misquote a couple of sentences in the book:

'Starting such a [book] is an adventure in itself. Who knows where it may lead or what might happen next? Take the first step [read the book], and enjoy the journey.'

Jennifer Newman
March 1997

1

Introduction

What the mind of man can conceive and believe it can achieve.

Napoleon Hill

This book has emerged from a firm belief in education 'happening' in the outdoors. The underlying concept is to get the pupils away from the formal environment of the classroom.

Although for many subjects, pupils and teachers it remains a secure and stimulating environment, there is an alternative: 'real' education can be found in the more natural surroundings out of doors.

It has to be accepted that not all our pupils are attracted to outdoor activities: there will always be 'indoor' animals. But behavioural studies indicate that although we are highly sophisticated creatures, we function in our world by retaining the basic instincts of survival found in the animals which we so admire, watch, study and lock up. The creation of sport, for example, as a 'hunt' substitute demonstrates our basic need to satisfy our primeval drive. The outdoors is our wilderness. The outdoors is where our ancient ancestors learned how to survive. The outdoors is where life presented dangers and challenges. The outdoors is where life began. The outdoors is why we have indoors.

My belief is that the outdoors presents challenges for today's children to learn about themselves as people.

The term OUTDOORS is used in a very broad sense and refers to an entirely non-academic situation which is open to the elements.

Naturally, the term ADVENTURE will mean something different to every person. Tackling the mighty white waters of the Zambezi will be a true adventure to some, whilst a casual bike ride through the countryside will be an adventure to others. Like beauty, adventure is in the eye of the beholder. This relative nature of the word leads me to attempt a definition. Not just a straightforward definition but one also relating to education:

'A state of mind that begins with uncertainty, fear or trepidation about the outcome of a journey and results in feelings of elation and satisfaction having completed that journey successfully.'

The aim of all teachers should be to guide successfully all their pupils through the journey of education at school to a safe and well-equipped start for the next phase of their journey through life.

By setting adventure in education as an area of the curriculum the aim for each participating pupil, with the help of their teacher, will be the successful completion of each and every task undertaken.

As each task is a joint venture, success is guaranteed.

Some may have reservations about the implementation of a new subject area such as this. Time is often at a premium and considering something new will always involve more time. Planning and preparation, becoming conversant with new ideas, learning the tasks so that they seem second nature, knowing what to look for, what to say, what to do. The whole situation can be daunting. I started from scratch but was so taken by the potential of adventure in education and the look of success on the faces of my pupils that I am now immersed, totally.

Well-run outdoor adventure courses are *great*. I take parties from school regularly. They are always tremendous fun; exciting; an 'adventure'. Sadly, they can result in elitism. Always it seems to be the same families who are able to send their sons and daughters away. As a result, through this book, I am attempting to bring the essence of such courses into the school and therefore into the curriculum. Following a recent OFSTED inspection our Physical Education department received a highly complimentary report stating how impressed the inspector was with all areas of the curriculum, and in particular with the fact that all five areas were being taught. That was encouragement indeed and added further fuel to the fire of my enthusiasm to develop the adventure course.

With the help of this collection of tasks an adventure programme can begin in *your* school.

Starting such a course is an adventure in itself. Who knows where it may lead or what might happen next? Take the first step and enjoy the journey.

Should any user of this book feel they can contribute to a further edition, please contact me. You may have some superb ideas that you are currently keeping to yourself or you may have some alternatives or changes to make to those included here.

The concept of adventure in education is such a wonderfully dynamic area that all schools should include it as a fundamental to every child's education, not just as part of the Physical Education programme.

It would be great if it became a part of our educational culture. Based in the theory of play, who can argue its existence and relevance?

I would also be happy to attend any school to run a day/half-day of activities to promote adventure – provided my Head agrees!

In any event, please call me at school, 01227 766263

Richard Andrews

'This is an early guide to the real world, to go logically and not just rush into things and mess them up.'

DAVID BANHAM, AGE 14

2

The Relationship with the National Curriculum

People who feel good about themselves produce good results.

Kenneth Blanchard

It is not my intention to become heavily bogged down in educational dogma or theory but since we are bound by the parameters of the National Curriculum it is perhaps important to allay certain fears or reservations some of us might have about where *Adventure in Education* really belongs. Initially, let's remind ourselves of *Why Physical Education*? I quote from the Department of Education and Science (August 1991) Physical Education for Ages 5–16 years:

> Physical Education is unique. It involves a variety of physical activities including sports, dance and outdoor pursuits, which are culturally valued and play a significant role in social life. Physical Education educates young people in and through the uses and knowledge of the body and its movement. It develops physical competence and enables pupils to engage in worthwhile physical activities; promotes development and teaches pupils to value the benefits of participation in physical activity while at school and throughout life and develops artistic and aesthetic understanding within and through movement. Physical Education also helps to establish self-esteem through the development of physical confidence and helps pupils to cope with both success and failure in competitive and cooperative physical activities. Physical Education also contributes to the development of problem-solving skills; the development of interpersonal skills; and the forging of links between the school and the community, and across cultures. Physical Education aims to develop physical competence so that pupils are able to move efficiently, effectively and safely and understand what they are doing. It is essentially a way of learning through action, awareness and observation.

In the hands of the right educationalist such aims move from being idealistic jargon towards being a very real proposition. Sadly, too much emphasis is placed on sport in schools. Thus a balanced curriculum is not maintained, sport becomes synonymous with physical education and all else is in danger of being forgotten. The uniqueness of our subject, whilst being a valuable asset, occasionally causes an identity crisis to occur. When this happens debates, arguments and discussions ensue. In the wake of heated words we find famous sports personalities making statements about the value of PE and of their experiences at school. Thus, the association is made: sport = PE However, these people are not the only product of a successful PE programme! It might be Richard Branson, Mother Teresa, the Reverend Ian Paisley; all are products of a sound physical education programme. Nick Leeson, who brought down Barings Bank, is probably the result of a sound mathematics curriculum! This is why Physical Education is such a unique and fundamental aspect of learning and it is why it is a statutory entitlement for all pupils between 5 and 16 years, including those with special needs.

So, to the National Curriculum. As a general requirement for Key Stages 1–4, it states that:

> Physical Education should involve pupils in the continuous process of planning, performing and evaluating. This applies to all areas of study. The greatest emphasis should be placed on the performance aspect of the subject.

Essentially the concern of this book is directed towards those pupils and staff involved in Key Stages 2–3, although that is not to preclude other stages. Indeed, the material here can be used far more widely. However, at Key Stages 2 and 3 **Outdoor and Adventurous Activities** (OAA) are included as areas of study, as they are in Key Stage 4, albeit at a more advanced level involving the pupils being away from the school premises. Whilst the tasks in this book can certainly be adapted and employed away from the school site, my intention is to provide a programme applicable to the National Curriculum which can be safely employed on-site. *Adventure in Education* happily involves all its participants in planning, performing and evaluation, for every single lesson. In its broadest aspects, then, we have an area of Physical Education which meets the requirements of the general aims of the National Curriculum.

OUTDOOR AND ADVENTUROUS ACTIVITIES AT KEY STAGE 2

A closer look at Key Stage 2 reveals the following:
Pupils should be taught:

- to perform outdoor and adventurous activities, eg orienteering exercise, in one or more different environment(s) such as playground, school grounds, parks, woodland, seashore;

- challenges of a physical and problem-solving nature, eg negotiating obstacle courses;

- using suitable equipment, eg gymnastic or adventure play apparatus, whilst working individually and with others;

- the skills necessary for the activities undertaken.

The tasks devised for *Adventure in Education*, their application and follow through, fulfil those requirements – with the one slight reservation being that not all schools will be in a position to hold classes off-site. To satisfy 'different environments' can therefore be a problem. This brings me back to the reason for making the tasks school-based. Naturally there could be nothing better than to get the pupils into a new environment and provide the challenges: there are many companies which survive and flourish for that sole purpose. But the expense of such a programme makes it prohibitive for many pupils and the guidelines of the DFE, therefore, cannot be easily met. Whilst I agree that a change of environment is important to the experiences of Key Stage 2 pupils, the real value for them comes in the form of the activities themselves.

OUTDOOR AND ADVENTUROUS ACTIVITIES AT KEY STAGE 3

Pupils should be taught:

- to perform at least one outdoor and adventurous activity, either on or off the school site;

- to apply the techniques and skills specific to the activity or activities undertaken;

- to plan and review the activity or activities undertaken;

- to perform at least one other outdoor and adventurous activity including, where possible, off-site work in unfamiliar environments;

- a variety of roles in each activity, including leadership, being led and sharing.

At this level, firstly, it appears that the expectation is to involve the pupils in climbing, canoeing or a similar activity normally associated with outdoor pursuits. In practical terms this again is not a possibility. Secondly, the area OAA may not be selected as an area of study for that very reason. Upon inspection of the relationship between AIE and the National Curriculum is clear and quite appropriate. *All* the tasks, by their very nature, are adventurous and can be employed outdoors (except those which are designed to employ gym bars and beams). So the first requirement, to perform at least one adventurous activity, is satisfied with interest and therefore meets the requirement of performing at least one other. Solving the tasks will require the application of techniques and skills of both the individual and the team. Planning and reviewing are at the very essence of the activities. By the very nature of the tasks each person will experience a variety of roles and share in the experience. At the hands of the teacher each pupil can be directed to adopt any role he or she deems fit and appropriate. The relationship is therefore complete. *Adventure in Education*, for Key Stage 2/3 pupils, is a route to explore the avenue of Outdoor and Adventurous Activities in an economical way. The aims of Physical Education itself, as a mother subject, are safely met, particularly with relevance to the development of problem-solving skills; of interpersonal skills; of the building of self-confidence and the value of working within a team framework in both competitive and cooperative situations. The value of this is actually enhanced as the subject is not viewed by pupils as 'regular PE'. The mould is broken and the association I spoke of earlier, sport = PE, is also removed. It is a whole new ball game – but with no balls! Naturally this has more appeal to those pupils who are turned off PE because they have never been good at soccer, netball, rugby, or any of the other 'traditional' school sports. I am, of course, biased in my opinions on the subject but in my experience of offering 'Adventure in Education' to our pupils the reception has been gratifying. When the weather is against us and the likelihood is that pupils will get cold, resistance has been met, but it is then down to the teacher to whip up enthusiasm and 'go-for-cold' or remain indoors and do the lesson. Either way, it is a team effort.

'Adventure is fun and training at the same time. What you do is fun and it is training you for the real world.'

RICHARD GARLICK, AGE 14

3

Why Adventure in Education?

Confining the idea of 'adventure' to the school premises will of course be
limited. But limited only by our imagination! What we can do with available
resources can be quite surprising. However, *why* should we be doing it anyway?

The benefits of a regular adventure programme, in which the pupils
participate in climbing, canoeing, abseiling and the like are numerous. I venture
to include these and others as benefits to a programme based entirely in school.

Below I have listed the reasons why we should consider spending more time
and money on **Adventure in Education**. Each area is simply a broad area of
interest to us as educators and therefore can be explored at will and, to a lesser
or greater extent, with the pupils we teach.

1. Communication Skills	13. Trust
2. Cooperation	14. Consideration for Others
3. Leadership	15. Persistence
4. Problem solving	16. Fairness
5. Thinking	17. Discipline
6. Non-competition or Competition	18. Planning
	19. Creativity
7. Self-concept	20. Responsibility
8. Team Building	21. Reflection
9. Decision Making	22. Physical Action – Strenuous/ Non-strenuous
10. Facing Challenges	
11. Adaptability	23. Initiative
12. Involvement For All	24. Endeavour

The list is quite comprehensive! Where else on the school timetable will you find
a subject which has so much to offer?

Much depends on the way the teacher handles the situations; the comments
made or not made. The whole process is very much a learning experience for all

concerned. Great insight can be gained of pupil relationships. Natural leaders are spotted quite easily (surprising ones at that!). The normally quiet ones of a group are seen to have something to say. The more vociferous types may find themselves suddenly out of their depth when they encounter a different type of problem. There will be those who cannot concentrate for the period of time necessary. Some groups will divide and there will be superb cohesion in others. The sheer dynamics of the situations are a delight to witness and a pleasure to help develop. There will be individual development as well as group development. The process remains open-ended and in that sense entirely special as a curriculum subject.

It ought to be said that whilst the PE teacher might well be the best placed person available to launch adventure it is by no means an area suited entirely to their knowledge or to that of their children. Indeed, in the Primary sector, any teacher, because of their acute knowledge of their pupils, would be ideal candidates to experiment with some of the tasks set out in this book.

'Adventure is also teaching you to be yourself. Try and show how you feel. Not to try and do what your best friend does but what *you* are. I find more confidence in myself, I may look a fool but I feel better after doing it.'

SIMON ROBINSON, AGE 13

4

Team Theory

Sayings remain meaningless unless they are embodied in habits.

Kahlil Gibran

Teams are at the very core of our society. No-one has ever done it alone! Whatever the 'it' may be, there will always be a team involved. A team is essentially more than one person, therefore it can comprise as few as two members or as many as hundreds, thousands or even millions. Whatever the number in a team it creates a dynamic social situation. The function of teams has been the subject of much psychological study in recent years, with the result that consultancies and training programmes are becoming quite ubiquitous.

In schools, where we are preparing the pupils for 'life', more emphasis should be placed upon teams. Team forming. Team building. Team spirit. Team dynamics. Team success. Teamwork.

Sadly, the mention of a 'team' in the school situation conjures up images of your typical Hockey or Soccer teams. The fact that the only teams that are given the spotlight are the sporting teams is a cultural problem. Sports teams receive the plaudits from the media and the word 'team' becomes synonymous with 'sport': not an erroneous assumption, as it is the essence of what teams actually do. They are a group of individuals who pool their own resources and skills, and work towards a common goal.

But teams flourish in all walks of society. Just about everybody we know is part of a team: at home, at work, at play. Getting things done requires teamwork. In education we ought to concern ourselves more readily with the importance of the *functioning* of the pupil, not only as an individual, but also as a team member.

Traditionally, in Physical Education, we employ sport as the medium for this ideal. Where we fail, and contrary to previous Sports Council endeavours, sport is *not* for all. This causes a few problems. I believe that through the careful nurturing and implementation of Adventure in Education (AIE), the values of teamwork can be enjoyed by all who participate and so effect a more well-rounded education.

As physical educationalists we will have limited knowledge of 'the study of teams' or 'group dynamics' but we can offer the contents of this book as a move in the right direction. Team theory can become very involved and go way beyond our immediate needs.

Consider the following:

- Team play
- Team build
- Team works.

The significance of 'play' in educational terms is, without any doubt, fundamental to learning. The warm-ups are basically games, therefore the teams 'play' together.

The next part of the process is the *building*. This occurs through 'playing' with ideas and 'doing' together. *Action* is the keynote.

'Works' has a dual meaning. Firstly, as the verb 'to work'. Secondly, as the successful result of a team effort.

As the process unfolds, in lessons, you will witness some fascinating behaviour patterns. A choice needs to be made as to whether or not to change the teams for each successive lesson. My advice would be to create different teams each time. In addition to the problem of solving the task, this will create new problems each time, making the process even more realistic.

From experience the group, according to its members, may or may not contain the following characters:

- a leader
- a worker
- a talker
- a follower
- an observer
- an arguer
- a peacemaker
- a questioner
- a summariser
- a joker.

Or there may be more than one of each. As individuals, they know they have a task to complete and yet they have to work together, perhaps for the first time. Your task, as a teacher, is to observe the process and in your debrief make them aware of what actually happened. Remember that *everyone* has something to offer – even though they may not be aware of that fact.

More considerations and factors that will ultimately affect the result and effectiveness of the team:

- A mix of individual personalities.

- The style of leadership.
- The size of the team.
- The environment – indoors/outdoors/hot/cold/wet/dry.
- Intelligence – banded groups/mixed ability.
- Self-concept – as individual/team member.
- Communication – between all members.
- Creativity and initiative – free/inhibited/criticised.
- Endeavour – enthusiasm/perseverance.

Less successful teams, following the debrief, can re-evaluate their shortcomings and make the necessary changes.

Thus we enter the learning cycle of **DOING – REVIEWING – LEARNING – APPLYING – DOING** and so on.

In terms of actual **team theory** the following can be regarded as a guideline. Whilst it is no way an exhaustive compilation it puts in focus the dynamics of a team situation. Analysing it further is a valuable and interesting exercise in itself but is not entirely essential at this level. To some extent even the information provided here goes beyond the need of the school situation but it serves a theoretical basis from which to start.

TEAM NEEDS

- Strong group identification
- Trust
- Shared responsibility
- Social activity
- Achievement
- Direction.

Strong group identification: The use of a war cry here is absolutely crucial. It has a binding effect. If you can encourage the team to create their own then the identity is home-grown and real.

Trust: Once the identity is formed it becomes important that each member begins to trust one another. I have included some trust games. You will know more.

Shared responsibility: As a team member each person has a responsibility to function within their team – at whatever level – to bring about the desired outcome.

Social activity: Social interaction is the lifeblood of successful teams. It must be stimulated between all members.

Achievement: This will be experienced through your verbal reporting in addition to actual performance. Tasks must therefore be set accordingly. Begin with level 1 and gradually move on. Achievement must come early to retain the levels of motivation and interest.

Direction: Stating the task clearly is going to be essential. It may need reiterating but not overexplained. Questions will arise at the outset but they need not be answered at this stage as confusion can be caused. Keep it simple. They should know exactly what they have to do. It will be down to them to find their own direction.

'It is interesting and different and also provides challenges of both mental and physical kinds so that all the pupils can join in.'

CHLOE LOVEJOY, AGE 13

'... it can also give you confidence in yourself, this can help you with a job interview.'

PAUL DAVIS, AGE 14

TASKS

- Purpose
- Aims
- Objectives
- Why?
- How?

Purpose: Having been given a relevant task, the team will understand that they have a common purpose. A team purpose. A meaning for the team to exist.

Aims. The aims will come from you and will vary according to the task set. In most cases the aim will be to complete the purpose, as a team, in a specific time period.

Objectives: These will be set by you and again will vary according to the nature of the task. They will include such ideas as physical contact, non-verbal communication, active communication, safety and so on.

Why and How?: The team will begin to ask these questions of the task and of their possible solutions. It is not always important for all members to ask the questions but input should be encouraged from all pupils, if not in asking, then in answering.

LEADERSHIP

Some teams will not have a natural leader but the team will soon realise that leadership is important, indeed essential, for any worthwhile action to occur. In most cases a leader will emerge. The characteristics of this person will vary from person to person and on how they view their role.

The Role of the Ideal Leader

Defining the task	– what it is and why you need to do it
Planning	– coordinate and check effectiveness
Briefing	– ensuring clear understanding of plan
Controlling	– dealing with issues, keeping focused
Supporting	– motivating and encouraging individuals
Informing	– keeping everyone in the picture/linking
Monitoring	– checking on progress
Reviewing	– relating success rate/feedback/appraisal.

Leadership styles

For convenience I have grouped together four main styles that I have witnessed in the process of AIE at school. It must be said that there are no hard and fast rules where children are concerned. Children have their own inimitable fashions and styles of dealing with situations. However, you will notice that some styles will emerge that may seem inappropriate to the task at hand. This can then become a point of discussion at the debrief stage – why wasn't that style working? What might have worked better?

● **Directing** – the leader provides specific instructions and supervises task completion.

● **Coaching** – the leader continues to direct and supervise the task completion and also explains decisions, asks for suggestions, and supports progress made.

● **Supporting** – the leader works with the team towards task completion and shares the responsibility for decision making with them.

● **Delegating** – the leader turns over responsibility for decision making and problem solving to the team.

Whilst the latter may seem rather extreme, I have witnessed it at first hand. The boy was a particularly strong character who held a certain 'position' in the group. More often than not the styles witnessed will fade across and overlap those described.

PROBLEM SOLVING

In the interests of brevity, I suggest that the following guidelines are used. Bear these in mind at all times since they may well form the basis of most debriefs. The pupils will need to be aware that a formula or process exists, yet without necessarily knowing the details. Hopefully you will notice an improvement as they get further into the course.

This Five Point Action Plan will not be the only route to a solution, but it can serve as a map and will naturally change according to varying styles of leadership. Notice that it turns full circle and so becomes a continuous dynamic process.

Five Point Action Plan

1. Identify — The task needs to be clearly stated and understood by *all* team members in terms of the actual aims and time. Agreement is necessary from all members.

2. Analyse — Check what equipment is available. View the opinions of the team. Review the facts. Check for any other resources – eg individual knowledge.

3. Generate Alternatives — Ideas and opinions from each member as to possible courses of action. Creative thought. Avoid value judgements.

4. Selection — Eliminate ideas through possible consequences and/or compliance with task parameters. Select the best option. Implement a test or rehearsal. Produce an agreed plan of action in which all members are aware of their role

5. Do it — Carry out the agreed plan of action. Review progress.
  ● Identify any problems
  ● Analyse
  ● Generate Alternatives
  ● Selection.
  ● *Do it!*

Brainstorming

Brainstorming is a technique which you could introduce, if the pupils are not already aware of it. Brainstorming is a technique which is frequently used in business when a group of individuals 'bounce' ideas off each other. This 'pooling' of creative thought processes often triggers inspired and previously unthought-of ways to tackle problems. Brainstorming could even be employed as a warm-up task. Set your group of pupils a topic or task, and give them a fixed time period to come up with ideas.

Brainstorming:

- enhances teamwork
- promotes creative thought and ideas
- produces ideas quickly
- produces a positive approach
- stimulates individual contribution.

> 'You discover new things and new skills, by discussing them first.'
>
> INDIA CARPENTER, AGE 13

Motivation

As in all areas of education, motivation is a prerequisite of learning. AIE is no exception. You will be naturally motivated by the subject, because it is an area in which you have an interest.

Since motivation is highly contagious it will rub off onto your pupils. What is important here is that throughout the tasks all pupils must be encouraged to motivate all pupils. This is teamwork in its basic form and will be a part of most, if not all, debriefs.

The theoretical principles mentioned here will remain sound for any team, whether it is together for a 50-minute lesson or a lifetime. The final principle to get across to the pupils is that:

what they are *doing* matters.

This is *powerplay*: play plus the power of purpose.

> 'Adventure is helping us become stronger and more efficient people.'
>
> SIMON LOVE, AGE 14

5

Making a Start –
The Adventure Begins

Destinations don't come to you.
Edward De Bono

A realistic start would be simply to experiment with one or two of the ideas contained here to get a feel for the concept of **adventure**.

There are quite a few tasks which require little or no equipment, making a start quite easy. I suggest this is an occasional one-off lesson. Starting in that way, prior to any major launch into the PE programme, will provide you with some experience as to what is required of you and the pupils. You will also need time to assess what equipment the school has and what might be needed to beg, borrow or steal (see Chapter 10: Help!).

The whole purpose of my programme is to bring outdoor pursuits into the school environment and so offer *all* the pupils something different, something exciting, something with which they can have fun. You will see that some of the tasks are nothing more than games. But the fact that they are presented as part of education creates a 'newness' in the minds of the pupils. Children nowadays seem to have forgotten how to play. Too much time is spent, in our modern world, in front of television screens, video screens or gameboy screens. Children are losing the ability to play. By bringing it back into an educational context, I feel the balance is being redressed to some extent and a worthwhile service is being provided.

When games come under the structure and supervision of a teacher, not by way of interference, but from someone who empathises and offers help, advice, encouragement and purpose, then the status of games is improved. There is enjoyment as well as learning.

THE ROLE OF THE TEACHER

The teacher's job is probably the hardest job of all. (You've all heard that before!) The reason it is hard in **adventure** is because there will be so many occasions when you'll want to scream and shout the answers and solutions to the children that the sheer frustration of keeping your mouth shut will be awesome!!!

So the job is crucial in the process.

In the first instance it is important to always bear in mind the main aim – **teambuilding**.

Secondly, you will need to bear in mind your own knowledge of the pupils you are dealing with. You will know from experience what sort of characters they are: how they might react to certain problems; what turns them on and off; who the stars are; who the loners are; who the jokers are; who the thinkers are; who *you* think the leaders are; who the doers are; who makes all the noise but no effort; who are the shy ones; the bold ones; the brave ones; the stupid ones; the silly ones? You have that knowledge which will have an affect on your approach.

Thirdly, you must enter into **adventure** with an open mind. Do not be tempted to pre-judge a reaction to a task or a reaction to a warm-up. At the start the pupils will assume that you know all there is to know, and that they are the ones in the dark. Trust in what you are doing – it works.

Finally, it is crucial that you show **enthusiasm** and your first task is to whip up the pupil's enthusiasm too. Put on a brave face and give it your best shot! (This is achieved quite quickly and easily by doing a **Team Scream** (see page 43).

This would probably follow a brief introduction to the new adventure programme. You might explain the importance of teamwork in just about everything we do in life. The family as a team. Your friends and you as a team. Your class as a team. Your school as a team. Your country as a team. The staff as a team.

Team are prevalent throughout all of society in many shapes and forms. So teams are important and we need to make sure that we all know how to function as a team.

You might also explain that teams are made up of individuals and those people, all of them, are important because each one will have something to offer.

Explain what the children will be doing and why.

So, to the **Team Scream**. This needs to be as loud and as outrageous as you can make it or bear it. I suggest you create your own and take it to the lesson with you as if it was a daily ritual!

Gather the class around you in a circle, perform your 'haka' boldly, trying not to show too much embarrassment, and enjoy the laughter which will follow. **YOU HAVE NOW STARTED**. The adventure has begun.

Remember the definition of adventure?

A word about the **Team Scream**. The All Blacks begin every game with their war cry (*haka*). So too should you start every adventure lesson with yours. Initially there will be slight resistance, especially from the shy ones, but stick with it because the bolder, louder pupils will look forward to it – you'll even get volunteers wanting to lead it. Do make sure *all* pupils join in.

The actual content of the scream should be brief and punchy with appropriate demonstrative actions. I'll attempt to describe mine, which is now used successfully not just at the start of every adventure lesson but also at the start of every school rugby match!

I am in the centre of the circle of pupils, unless there is a volunteer to take that position.

'AAAAARRRGGHHHHHH!' is screamed as loud as we can whilst at the same time we run ferociously on the spot. After about three seconds we stop and immediately shout 'OOO–OOO-OOO' while punching the air with our right hands three times. Immediately following this we bend forward at the waist, stretch our arms to the centre of the circle, wave our hands, walk backwards calling out 'TEEEAAAAMMMM'.

The three distinct phases, which flow together, have three different sounds and three different actions. It looks good and more importantly, having completed it, it feels good! It marks the start of our teambuilding. Yours will too.

Having done the **Team Scream** it then becomes essential that the pace of the lesson continues at a workmanlike speed. If enthusiasm allows you to race away – so will the kids. *Controlled* enthusiasm is the order of the day.

Preparation

Preparation is essential. You must know exactly the 'what's', 'where's', 'how's' and 'who's'. If any equipment needs setting up then it must be done prior to the lesson. Without this preparation the pace will be lost and so too the purpose of your lesson.

As an experienced teacher you will know the value of being prepared. As an experienced teacher I know that you have the ability to improvise in circumstances when time has been at a premium, not allowing the fullest preparation of lessons. The same can occur in adventure. Improvisation is very much a part of the teaching technique because you will be responding to some new and exciting stimuli.

To a certain extent, because of the three years of 'doing' adventure I improvise quite a lot, with equipment, ideas and pupils. It is a natural course of development, but in the first instance aim for success.

TASK LEVELS

All the tasks have been graded to help with their use: **1 (easy), 2 (moderate), 3 (hard)**, or **4 (very hard)**. You might find it helpful to begin with all easy tasks before moving on to others. I use the easy tasks as an introduction to the lessons or as a warm-up. Then I find a slightly harder task and, time allowing, finish with something more taxing. Individual differences will determine exactly what you do. Much also depends on the level of the group. Again only you will know exactly where to pitch the level.

Aims and objectives

Every task has the main aim of **team building**.

However, the objectives can differ for each task depending on whether or not you decide to use a thematic approach, selecting an area which you think a particular group needs. You will, of course, be able to angle the attack to any task which suits your needs. In the table on page 102, I have indicated which tasks are most suitable for developing either group skills or individual skills. This is to aid with planning on a theme basis, should you need it.

Whilst the benefits of such a course are extremely wide and varied the attempt to reduce the objectives to only two categories is simply achieved. What is not so simple is the breakdown of the tasks into more closely-defined objectives. Highlighting a specific objective such as 'persistence' or 'self concept' is not so easy because all the tasks will have some element of all those listed as the reasons why we should be incorporating *Adventure in Education* into the curriculum.

You can apply your own emphasis in the lesson so that any adaptations can be made.

'The Team Scream is not a silly thing to do; it is getting everyone to be part of the group.'

RICHARD GOULD, AGE 13

6
Debriefs

It is absolutely essential, particularly in the early stages, that, following the completion of the lesson, time is set aside for a debrief. I would actually recommend such a session immediately following each task, but the flow of the lesson is just as crucial so really it comes down to your teaching style.

The whole idea behind a debrief is quite simple. A debrief makes the pupils aware of what they actually achieved and how they achieved it. It is important to not use negatives in any discussions. No team fails at any task; they just succeed at different levels.

That may seem trite and unimportant but in psychological terms to allocate a failure label to any group or individual, whether said in humour or not, can have a lasting effect and will keep returning to haunt some people.

Everyone succeeds at adventure.

At this stage you need to attempt to bring everyone into the discussion. There will, of course, be those who want to dominate the input, just as they may have

---

A Typical Debrief

A typical debrief must include the following:

- Immediacy – either following the task or lesson
- What was the task?
- Was the team successful?
- Why?
- Was it enjoyable? If not, why not?
- Who had ideas?
- Who was quiet?

- Who worked?
- Who did what?
- Did anyone do anything they didn't want to do?
- How could all problems be approached?
- How might that help problems in everyday life?

---

dominated the task performance. Let them have their say but also make them aware that their behaviour now was just the same during the task.

By asking:

- How?
- What?
- Why?
- When?
- Who?
- Where?

you will cover all that needs to be covered.

On the opposite page you will see the sorts of questions that need to be asked. Again your experience and natural abilities will come to bear on the situation.

The discussion can be very open but needs to be led by you down any channel of thought you want to go down. You will be aware of the aims and objectives you have set, so bear those in mind during the debrief. Bring out those areas and again make your pupils aware of them.

They will undoubtedly have fun in performing the task but they must realise the significance of what they have just achieved as a team who have never done anything before together.

During the task make notes as to who was criticising others and ask the class whether they thought that type of attitude was productive. Basically you have a choice of whether to deal with it there and then or wait for the debrief. My guideline would be to wait and adopt a silent approach until the tasks are complete and then launch headlong into certain individuals who drastically hindered the team's performance. The team will know anyway, but you should reaffirm the team's feelings and let the class know that you haven't missed a thing.

The more difficult problems need the solution explained in case it wasn't discovered successfully. Probably you will find that the teams will want to redo the task all over again. And why not? Let them! They will formulate opinions about the difference between the two solutions: theirs and yours. Theirs, of course, will be better.

Bring the debrief to a conclusion. The entire affair should not last more than 10–15 minutes. The emphasis must be on the tasks, not the debrief, because that is where the learning takes place; the debrief simply provides the consolidation and reinforcement.

'Helping each other is what it is all about. Thinking positively about each other. Listening to each other is teamwork.'

ANTHONY LEES, AGE 13

? How...	? What...	? Why...	? When...	? Who...	? Where...
could the team have improved their performance?	would have made the difference?	did that work?	did you realise that you were succeeding?	did the team not listen to?	were you?
could the task have been completed differently?	would have happened if...?	was so and so doing what he was doing?	should the discussion have been?	else could have done that job?	would it have been better placed?
can teams function more efficiently?	do you think about the way so and so told everybody what to do?	was it that things went well?	is a team really a team?		did you go then?

7

Burdens

Results not excuses.
Richard Andrews

A burden is an extra problem which the team must contend with during the course of the task performance.
In this chapter I have listed the types of burdens which I use. As you progress you will think of others.

- **Blindfolds** – use on any number of people.

- **An object** – a *fragile object*, like an egg, which must remain intact throughout the task;
  – a *heavy weight*, like a bench or two or three medicine balls which must not touch the ground at any time;
  – a *liquid*, such as a container of water without a top. As much water must be kept in the container and measured at the end to evaluate the loss in terms of points.

- **Points** – a point system immediately creates competition and puts the team under pressure. Points can be awarded at the end for successfully completing a task, with deductions for errors, ie touching the ground (the team thinking they got away with it). At this point you can employ the non-doers of the lesson. Those pupils who have notes excusing them or have forgotten their kit. They can be gainfully employed as judges and so remain involved in the lesson.
  Points can be awarded at the beginning as a total with deductions being made during the course of the task. You can ask the teams to keep their own score – identify their honesty by comparing the score with that of the judges or yours. Award more or deduct more as the case may be.

- **Time** — place a time limit on certain tasks.

- **Multiples** — set a number of tasks for the teams to complete, moving directly from one to the next without a break. This is a real test of initiative. Depending on how you word the instructions and what tasks you set, the team's reaction to such a multiple problem is fascinating. Some remain as a team, working on each task as they meet it – other teams break to work on other tasks simultaneously. It's a good one.

- **Memory** — give the team a saying to remember and repeat upon the completion of the task.

- **Envelope** — provide the teams with a sealed envelope and explain that it can be opened but points will be lost if it is. The envelope is sealed in such a way that opening it will be an irreversible action. Inside is a blank piece of paper.

- **Items** — during the course of the task certain items must be found and presented at the finish; eg a piece of elastoplast, an oak leaf, a piece of chalk. The variety of 'burdens' is endless.

'... it is a good change. Something a bit more challenging. It helps you develop better thinking.'

THOMAS HOLDSWORTH, AGE 14

8

Troubleshooting

A clever man commits no minor blunder.
Johann von Goethe

Well, what can go wrong?

The fact that you planned the lesson so perfectly means that all sorts of things could happen!

Before anything happens in the lesson *safety* must be your first priority. The tasks are not dangerous provided control is maintained. Because of the newness of the subject matter and its similarity to games and play the atmosphere which pervades is lightheartedness as well as escapism. I say escapism because it is different from the normal lesson. It is like giving pupils a new toy for the first time. The novelty creates excitement and with it potential hazards.

A word here about newness. I only teach **adventure** to Year 8 and Year 9 pupils in one term for a six-week block. So the mixed groups receive a total of twelve weeks before they move into 'options' in Year 10. The hope is that Outdoor Pursuits is selected following the course in adventure. Inexplicably, so far, it has been more girls than boys who opt for the Outdoor Pursuits.

What I hope I avoid by keeping the introduction to adventure brief and in two short sharp bursts is the potential problem of staleness. In this format, the ideas come from the pupils as well and the response is good to great.

So what can go wrong? And what do you do when it does?

In fact, there is not a lot that can go wrong – barring some pupil breaking a leg or neck – but then you know what to do with that situation anyway.

Start in the way I suggest. Experiment with one or two simple games first and get the 'feel' for what goes on. You will be able to move on confidently from there. You will be able to pick up the vibes from the pupils as to what they think and so plan the next move.

Ideas will come to you as they work/play for the next progression without you having to come back to this book. You will think of improving some tasks – ways of modifying it – employing another piece of equipment – removing a piece – and so on. The whole concept is a never-ending dynamic learning curve.

Keep in mind goals – *teambuilding*.

'It has to be both serious and funny. But as someone starts being stupid, put them in their place because it's your team, look after it.'

DAVID BANHAM, AGE 14

9
Help!

**The world is full of willing people. Some willing
to work, the rest willing to let them.**
Robert Frost

Most of the equipment employed in the tasks will be part of your stock lists.
Hopefully!

If you take a good look around your school – in those cupboards, sheds and
garages that no-one ever goes in any more. At the back of rooms that you
cannot normally reach. Under the stage. In boxes that have been closed since
those other boxes were put on top of them; you'll be pleasantly surprised at
what you might find and wonder why you haven't looked before!

PEOPLE AT SCHOOL WHO CAN HELP

- The **caretaker** – here is a person, if he is anything like ours, who will
  bend over backwards to help. His store and stock cupboards, sheds and
  outbuildings are stacked with a multitude of 'bits' that would grace any
  Boot Fair and fetch a fortune. He would be the first person to approach.
  The likelihood is that, should he not be able to help, he will know a man
  who can. What must be avoided is going to the expense, in monetary
  terms, of getting something only to hear him say those awful words 'Why
  didn't you ask me?'

- The **CDT Department** – these people can make anything out of anything.
  They can change items from being useful into highly functional
  equipment. I asked the department at my school to make the wooden
  puzzles for some of the tasks. It took some time but they arrived and
  have been worth their weight in gold ever since. If you haven't a nodding
  acquaintance with the head of this department yet – get nodding.

- The **PTA** – should you feel a need to buy anything, then a word with the
  chairman to see if any funds are available wouldn't go amiss.

- The **Parents** – to my mind here is a resource which is entirely unexploited.

Apply the latest 'buzz' word – *networking*. It simply means ask someone to ask someone to ask someone. In this way you get to reach loads of people just by asking one. The number of parents who are naturally keen to help and sympathetic to the school's needs is endless. Many, I am certain, will find a way of helping.

OTHER SOURCES OF HELP

- **BT** – make discreet enquiries and you will find the man who looks after old telegraph poles. He *does* exist. A small purchase price can be negotiated.

- **Local Council** – the Highways Department will be able to furnish you with what I call 'mine-tape'. This is the red and white or orange and white plastic tape used to mark off roadworks between cones (which you will also be able to get). They come in many different sizes and they're heavy too.

- **Sailing Clubs/Docks/Harbours** – all of these places will have, hopefully, discarded ropes of many types. Docks and harbours in particular have many just lying around. You need only find the right person to contact. Old ships' hawsers are great and very versatile. Heavy, but just what you need.

- **Pubs/Breweries/Dairies** – You will be able to acquire an abundance of various types of crates. Perhaps even some old barrels.

- **The Forces** – since they are extremely helpful towards education and they will recognise your **adventure** programme as a scaled-down version of their command tasks used in officer selection and training, I am sure they will oblige with anything they can.

You'll be surprised how quickly bits and pieces can accumulate when you have a mind to collect them.

> '
In the team every person has a job to do, each one of these is equally important.'
>
> DI STEWART, AGE 13

THE TASKS

I pay less attention to what men say.
I just watch what they do.
Andrew Carnegie

Notes

1. Because the primary objective of *Adventure in Education* is teambuilding, every task included here will involve teamwork, ie the development of group skills. The individual must accept the concept of being a team member. This may well require a shift in thinking, as more often than not pupils work individually at school. What is often overlooked is the fact that group skills are also valuable in developing *individual* skills.

   What you should see, with respect to individual development, is:

   - improved **communication** via listening and questioning (being precise with language is important for progress; avoids confusion and possible conflict);

   - more **confidence** by responding to instructions and ideas; problem-solving; using initiative. Simply *thinking with confidence* is a step forward for many pupils;

   - improved **self-discipline**, through facing challenges which might not otherwise have presented themselves; and above all

   - the development of **trust**, from interaction in a team environment. Without this the team cannot exist.

   The Task Information Summary in the Appendix indicates which of the tasks may be particularly valuable in developing individual, as well as group, skills.

2. The tasks in Task Level 1 (easy) can be used as warm-ups for all the tasks at other levels. They need no planning time or debrief when used in conjunction with Task Level 4 (very hard).

3. Warm-ups are aimed at achieving one or a combination of the following:

- Fun
- Creating atmosphere
- Team spirit
- Physical contact
- Cooperation
- Communication
- Initiative
- Creative thinking
- Teambuilding.

4. **Task Cards**. These tasks can be copied onto card and simply handed to each team when necessary. This may avoid the teacher being plied with too many questions, maybe causing confusion.

5. **Red Herrings**. These are simply extra pieces of equipment unnecessary to be able to complete the task – they act as decoys.

6. **Diagrams**. Where precise set-up of equipment is needed a detailed diagram is provided.

7. **Timing**. Timing for each task can be varied according to ability/ intelligence/time constraints/degree of set-up/weather conditions/distance/ nature of task/number of pupils/level of assistance needed.

8. **Safety**. There must be an emphasis on safety on all times. The only potentially dangerous task is Tall Order, but of course accidents can happen at the most unlikely times. Remember: CONTROL = SAFETY.

9. The whole process should be dynamic and evolutionary. Be guided by your experience and instincts when modifying the tasks, or creating new ones. Indeed, encourage your pupils to think up their own progressions and/or burdens whenever possible.

Level 1 – Easy

'Warm-ups': Creating the
Atmosphere

Name:	ISLANDS
Group Size:	16+
Level of Activity:	Active
Equipment:	Four or five frisbees
Level of Set-up:	Low

Command Task:
Starting from anywhere, on the command 'GO' the group must get to a frisbee and touch it without touching anyone else. Once they have reached the frisbee they must remain in contact with it **but no-one else**: only the frisbee.

Progressions:
- Remove a frisbee each time, so that it becomes increasingly difficult not to touch another person.
- See how many people can touch a frisbee without touching each other.
- Create a school record.

Islands

Name:	SKIN THE SNAKE
Group Size:	9–15
Level of Activity:	Active
Equipment:	None

Command Task:

Teams stand in a line. Each person puts their right hand through their legs to grasp the left hand of the person behind. On the command 'GO' the person at the back of the line must sit down and the team pass over them backwards, 'skinning the snake'. First team to finish without breaking grips stands up.

Progressions:

- Play in reverse, the teams 'skinning' the snake from back to front.
- Create a snake using: the whole class;
the whole year group;
the whole school.

Skin the Snake

Name:	UP AND DOWN
Group Size:	16+
Level of Activity:	Active
Equipment:	None

Command Task:

Linking hands they must arrange themselves so that each alternate person is supported with their feet off the ground for 30 seconds. They must not break their grip once it is decided who needs to go next to whom. The solution is so easy but the chances are they will make life difficult by looking for a complicated answer.

Progressions:

● None.

Name:	TEAM SCREAM
Group Size:	Any
Level of Activity:	Very active
Equipment:	None

Command Task:

The group must form a circle, hands to the centre, waving them as they begin a really loud AAARRRGH. All clap hands once, jump in the air and shout WWOOOOO!

ie Aaaaarrrrgh! (CLAP) Wwooooo! (timing is essential to get the real effect). A great confidence booster!

Progressions:

- Break into smaller groups which can make up their own team scream.

Name:	KNOTS
Group Size:	1–8
Level of Activity:	Passive
Equipment:	None

Command Task:
The group forms a circle, shoulder to shoulder, placing hands to the centre. Each person grabs somebody's hand with their left hand and another person's hand with their right hand. They must work together to untangle the knot without breaking their grip.

Progressions:
- None.

Knots

Name:	ALL CHANGE
Group Size:	1–8
Level of Activity:	Passive
Equipment:	Gym bench per team
Level of Set-up:	Medium

Command Task:

All stand on the bench. Number off consecutively. Without leaving the bench, they must reverse the numerical order in which they are standing.

Progressions:

- Turn the bench upside down (!)

Name:	ALL IN ORDER
Group Size:	9–15
Level of Activity:	Passive
Equipment:	None

Command Task:
In teams, see if they can arrange themselves in order of height.

Progressions:
- Order of birthdays.
- Alphabetical order of Christian names.
- Alphabetical order of surnames.
- Order of house numbers.
- Alphabetical order of street names.

Name:	HEAD DOWN ROUND AND ROUND
Group Size:	1–8
Level of Activity:	Very active
Equipment:	A large cone (traffic or games)
Level of Set-up:	Low

Command Task:

Each person, one at a time, must get to the cone, places their hands on the top of the cone followed by their head and then run around the cone ten times without coming off. Run back to the start for the next person to go. The aim is to be the first team to finish.

Progressions:

- None – fun in itself.

Head Down Round and Round

Name:	BUG TUG
Group Size:	1–8, 9–15 or 16 +
Level of Activity:	Active
Equipment:	None

Command Task:
Ask pupils to stand back to back in pairs, clasping hands between legs. On the command 'pull' – they must try and pull the other person towards them.

Progressions:
- Building up to groups of fours, sixes and so on, by standing in lines and clasping the hands of the people either side of them, their hands between their legs.
- Once in position move forwards or backwards as an entire team (no competition).
- Move in a lengthwise direction – as a team.

Bug Tug and progression

Name:	ROUND THE BARREL
Group Size:	9–15
Level of Activity:	Active
Equipment:	One or two barrels/large plastic rubbish bins
Level of Set-up:	Low

Command Task:

The group forms a circle around the barrel, clasping hands. They must then move about in order to make someone touch the barrel. Whoever touches the barrel is out. When only two people remain they each clasp one hand across the barrel and attempt to pull each other out.

Progressions:

● None.

Round the Barrel

Name:	CATCH TAIL
Group Size:	9–15
Level of Activity:	Very active
Equipment:	Two coloured team bands
Level of Set-up:	Low

Command Task:

In two teams, get pupils to form a chain by placing their hands on the waist of the person in front of them. The front person must try and catch their own tail. The aim is to avoid the tail being caught.

Progressions:

- Front person to catch other team's tail.
- Change positions (ie, head becomes tail and vice versa).

Name:	PLATES OF MEAT
Group size:	1–8
Level of Activity:	Active
Equipment:	A marked area, anything which will act as a red herring
Level of set-up:	Low

Command task:
No-one must come out of the area. As a team they must find a safe way to arrange themselves so that their feet do not touch the ground.

Progressions:
• None.

Name:	DESERT ISLAND
Group size:	16+
Level of Activity:	Active
Equipment:	Five gym mats
Level of Set-up:	Medium

Command Task:
On the command 'GO', they must find a mat and stand on it.
No-one must be touching the floor.

Progressions:
• Remove a mat and repeat until only one mat remains.
• Place a piece of wood 1m x 1m on a crate (for smaller groups) instead of using a mat.

Level 2 – Moderate

Team Play

Name:	CONNECT FOUR
Group Size:	9–15
Level of Activity:	Active
Equipment:	Two different coloured sets of bibs Six channels marked out
Level of Set-up:	Medium

Command Task:

Give each team a numerical order. Number 1 from either team moves as far down any channel they like. Number 1 from the other team then does the same. Each team proceeds in numerical order. The aim is to 'connect' four people from the same team in a horizontal, vertical or diagonal line, while the other team moves to prevent this.

Progressions:

- Silence – gives practice in non-verbal communication.

Name:	PEOPLE SNAKE
Group Size:	9–15
Level of Activity:	Active
Equipment:	Uprights, two long ropes (or many skipping ropes), two large hula hoops (tied in position or held)
Level of Set-up:	High

Command Task:
Spread your pupils evenly along the length of the rope and ask them to pick it up. Without letting go, changing their position or allowing the rope to touch the ground they must go through the hoop to the finishing line without the rope or any member of the team touching it. If so, they have to start again.

Progressions:
- Alter the height of the hoop.
- Alter the size of the hoop.
- Alternate pupils to be blindfolded.
- Alternate pupils to go backwards.
- Make up several teams and have a competition.

Name:	BLIND ALLEY
Group Size:	Pairs
Level of Activity:	Active
Equipment:	Blindfolds, anything to create an obstacle course
Level of Set-up:	High

Command Task:

The first leader of the pairs is to guide the blindfolded person verbally around the obstacle course safely. He or she cannot touch the blindfolded person. Once completed the other half of the pair guides them on their return trip.

Progressions:

- Complicate the course with more obstacles.
- Avoid the pupils seeing the course prior to tackling it.
- Create a point system for competition.
- Get pupils to communicate via coded messages.

Name:	TEAM SKI
Group Size:	1–8, 9–15, 16+
Level of Activity:	Active
Equipment:	Three sets of team skis, ie each ski to be a length of strong wood/plank having toe-bindings attached for four people along its length. The bindings need to be strong material/webbing and secured firmly to the edges with nails or heavy duty staples. Ropes can be tied around the plank to form handles.
Level of Set-up:	Medium

Command task:
Divide into teams of up to four, each team taking it in turn to complete a circuit as quickly as possible.

Progressions:
- Do several circuits.
- Build a set of team skis for six, eight or more people!!!
- Create an obstacle course.

Name:	BLANKET BALL
Group Size:	1–8
Level of Activity:	Very active
Equipment:	A piece of material and a ball per team, (large towel/blanket/ground sheet), (football/volleyball)
Level of Set-up:	Medium

Command Task:

Using the blanket see how many consecutive times each team can successfully catch and launch the ball.

Progressions:

- Play a game over a net.
- Suspend a hula hoop vertically at a convenient height. Teams try to throw the ball through the hoop to each other.
- Use a basketball hoop and backboard, or a netball post and net.

Name: DAMSEL IN DISTRESS

Group Size: 1–8

Level of Activity: Active

Equipment: A paved area as a chessboard

Level of Set-up: Low

Command Task:
Using only the Knight's move they must construct a safe path of squares to rescue the damsel. Number the pupils 1–8 and move in numerical order. Once they have created a safe path of squares they must stay in that position.

Progressions:
- Introduce a burden.
- Reduce the team size to five (it still works).

Damsel in distress

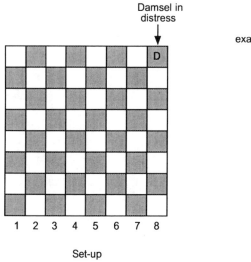

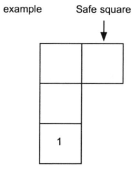

Set-up

Safe area

Name:	RAT UP A DRAINPIPE
Group Size:	1–8
Level of Activity:	Active
Equipment:	A short length of downpipe, a 1.5 litre plastic bottle filled with water, two long ropes, also anything as a red herring
Level of Set-up:	Medium

Command Task:
Mark out an area of any shape or size and set down the bottle and downpipe inside so that pupils cannot reach them. The downpipe must be firmly set into the ground. As a team they must get the plastic bottle into the downpipe without entering the area or physically touching the bottle.

Progressions:
- Introduce a burden, eg blindfolds.

Name:	RAFT RACE
Group Size:	1–8
Level of Activity:	Active
Equipment:	3 gym benches
Level of Set-up:	Medium

Command Task:
Set the benches as a raft ie: next to each other. With the team on the raft they must get themselves as quickly as possible from a to b (defined by you) without touching the ground in between. **Note**: Space the benches so that it is possible for the team to reach over them.

Progressions:
- None.

Name:	STUMPED
Group Size:	1–8
Level of Activity:	Active
Equipment:	Three milk crates/beer crates, 4m plank, 2m plank, tentpegs (to secure crates to the ground), two school benches, laid out as shown
Level of Set-up:	Medium

Command Task:

Pupils must work as a team to get across from the start to the finish without touching the ground. Should anyone or anything touch the ground then the team starts again.

Progressions:

- Provide a burden, eg carry an egg, a bucket of water, or blindfold someone.

- Construct multiple numbers of stumps or a 'minefield' – bring other planks into play.

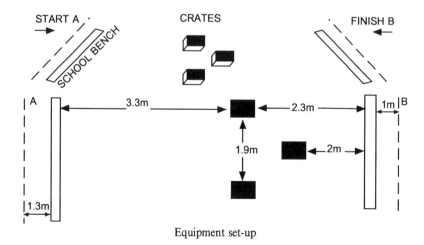

Equipment set-up

Name:	TOTAL 30
Group Size:	16–19 exactly (but the whole group can work)
Level of Activity:	Passive
Equipment:	None

Command Task:

Number off 1–19. Pupils then form a circle around number 10, arranging themselves so that everyone opposite each other, including number 10, adds up to a total of 30.

Progressions:

• None.

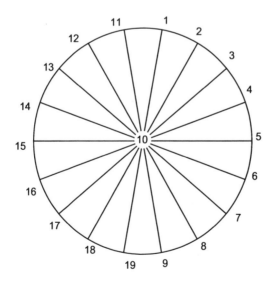

Total 30 – solution

Name: IT ALL ADDS UP

Group Size: 9 exactly

Level of Activity: Passive

Equipment: Marked out area, equilateral triangles

Level of Set-up: Low

Command Task:
Number each person in each team. The team has to arrange itself around the triangle, two on each side and one at each apex so that the total on each side adds up to 17.

Progressions:
- None.

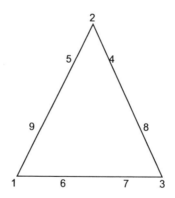

It All Adds Up – solution

Name:	POLE TO POLE
Group Size:	1–8
Level of Activity:	Active
Equipment:	Telegraph pole or builder's scaffolding plank, with a fixed pivot (eg an overturned tree stump) at a point about a quarter of the way along its length. (Note: in the interests of safety the telegraph pole should have a fixed pivot point at about one third along its length – not a crate as illustrated
Level of Set-up:	High

Command Task:
Standing on the pole or plank, the team must balance the pole in a horizontal position.

Progressions:
- Get the pupils to think of one.

Name:	HIGH AND DRY
Group Size:	1–8
Level of Activity:	Active
Equipment:	Two long ropes, bucket of water, red herrings (eg plank, pole, hoop, ball)
Level of Set-up:	Medium

Command Task:
The bucket of water must be removed from a marked area without any person crossing the line and going into the area (this includes reaching over!).

Progressions
• Have all pupils blindfolded except one.

Name:	ROUND TABLE
Group Size:	1–8
Level of Activity:	Active
Equipment:	A school dining table per team (not too wide), or a gym horse
Level of Set-up:	Low

Command Task:

Starting with the first person on the table, each person must travel around the table, from the top to underneath and back to the top again. Get as many people as you can around the table in five minutes. No help must be given to the person travelling other than holding the table securely at each corner. You must not touch the ground – only the table.

Progressions:

• None.

Name:	BLOCKS, LENGTHS, DOWELS
Group Size:	1–8
Level of Activity:	Passive
Equipment:	Six short lengths of square wood, seven short lengths of dowel, six rectangular blocks of wood
Level of Set-up:	Medium

Command Task:
(Each set to a different team.) The shapes of wood must be arranged so that all the blocks touch each other, all the lengths touch each other and all the dowels touch each other.

Progressions:
• Reduce the time periods allowed to complete the task.

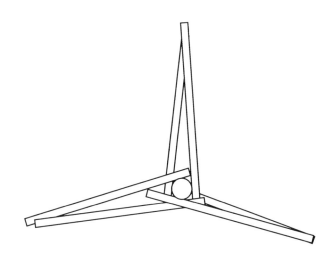

A solution to 'Dowels'

Name:	BLIND SHAPE
Group Size:	1–8, 9–15, 16+
Level of Activity:	Passive
Equipment:	Long rope, equal number of blindfolds per person
Level of Set-up:	Low

Command Task:
With blindfolds on, the team(s) must try to form a square.

Progressions:
- Form a pentagon.
- Form a hexagon.
- Form an octagon.
- Form a circle!!!

Name:	RIVER CROSSING
Group Size:	1–8
Level of Activity:	Active
Equipment:	As many different size hoops as possible, each team to be given the same number of different sizes
Level of Set-up:	Medium

Command Task:
These hoops are their stepping stones to get them across the river. Should their feet get wet, by coming out of the hoops, then the team starts again. Only four feet are allowed on any one 'stone' at a time.

Progressions/variations:
- Take a hoop away and repeat, then do this again with one less hoop.
- Number the individual members of the team – odds cannot travel with evens.
- Only an odd number of feet allowed in a hoop.
- Three cannibals and three priests on opposite sides of a river, all want to cross to the other side. Using one hoop as a boat which can take only two people, the aim is to get them all across safely, without leaving more cannibals than priests on either side.
- One person is a farmer, another is a chicken, another a fox, another a sack of corn. The boat only takes the farmer and one other. Everything has to get across safely without the fox eating the chickens or the chickens eating the corn.
- Five cannibals, five priests, three in a boat. Only one of each can row. There is no trust between the two groups. At no time can there be unequal numbers, either in the boat or on the shore. Can the groups get across safely?

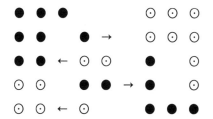

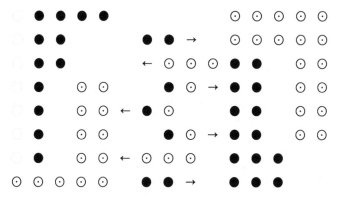

Solutions to Cannibals and Priests
and Farmer and Animals

Name: CLUE ORIENTEERING
Group Size: 1–8
Level of Activity: Very active
Equipment: School ground maps, markers, clue sheets
Level of Set-up: Medium

Command Task:

Using the clues provided, the group has to complete the course as quickly as possible.

The idea is to 'plant' clues around the school premises which lead the teams eventually back to your starting point. Try to provide each group with a different set of clues. This will ensure the entire class is working at the same time. However, it will make extra demands on your time and organisation. The clues will relate to places around the outside of the buildings, preferably not too close to the buildings themselves. You don't want complaints from other teachers about your adventurers!

Example
Clue 1: *A place to put a ball, using your foot, to win.* This will lead your group to a goal post. Once they have found the correct one they will discover the next clue.

Clue 2: *A tree which gives away 'one-ers' and 'two-ers'.* This will take them to the chestnut tree.

And so on.

Note: Remember to distinguish, in some way, between clues for the different groups. This could be colour-coded or alphabetical. Also ensure that each group, upon discovering a 'wrong' clue, *leaves it alone*. You can include compass bearings provided that you have covered it in a previous lesson!!!

Progressions:
• Harder clues.
• Introduce a burden.

Name:	SHAPES
Group Size:	1–8
Level of Activity:	Passive
Equipment:	Hexagon, octagon, circle, letter 'H', each one painted a different colour and sliced into about 6 or 8 pieces (ideally as large as possible and made from wood)
Level of Set-up:	Medium

Command Task:
To make the required shape as quickly as possible from a random pile of pieces.

Progressions:
- Set shorter time periods to complete the shape.

Name:	MINI ASSAULT COURSE
Group Size:	1–8
Level of Activity:	Active
Equipment:	Whatever is available
Level of Set-up:	High

Command Task:
To complete the course in the quickest time possible.

Progressions:
- All except one person blindfolded – no body contact, verbal instructions only taken from the person not blindfolded.
- Carrying a measured amount of water.
- Carrying an egg or eggs.

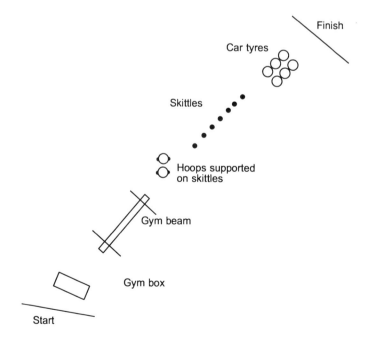

LEVEL 3 – HARD

TEAM BUILD

Name:	BLIND TRAIL
Group Size:	1–8
Level of Activity:	Active
Equipment:	A long length of mine-tape (roadworkers tape) or 20 metres of light string that will not break, blindfolds for everyone except the leader
Level of Set-up:	High

Command Task:
As a team, follow the tape wherever it goes, from start to finish without removing the blindfolds.

Note: *Blind Trail* is ideal for setting among a wooded area of the school grounds. The more challenging the route – over a low fence or wall, through a tunnel, under or over branches etc – the more exciting the result.

Progressions:
- Connect each person by a rope.
- Have alternate pupils going backwards (take care!).
- Increase the size of the team.

Name:	DRY WATER PADDLE
Group Size:	1–8
Level of Activity:	Active
Equipment:	Canoe, two oildrums/large rubbish bins, four large cones, four tennis balls, crash mat (not a gym mat), set of paddles
Level of Set-up:	High

Command Task:
Set up as illustrated. Each team member must take his/her turn in the canoe and knock off the balls with the paddle blades. All four balls must be removed before the next person has a turn. Hands must be kept in the same place on the paddles throughout the task.

Progressions:
- Marks can be made on the paddle blades using coloured tape. Balls can be knocked off only by the specified colour-marked areas of the paddle. The nearer the marks are to the blades, the harder the task.

Name:	26 IN LINE
Group Size:	9–15
Level of Activity:	Passive
Equipment:	Marked area(s)
Level of Set-up:	Low

Command Task:

Number a team 1–12. They must try to arrange themselves so that the total among each line is 26.

Progressions:

- None.

Marked area

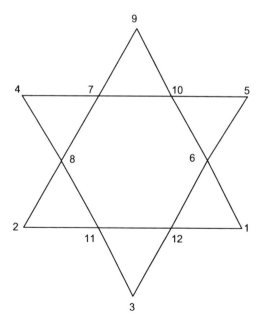

26 in Line – solution

Name:	TEAM TRANSFER
Group Size:	1–8
Level of Activity:	Very active
Equipment:	Long rope, three rounders poles, four gym mats, gym box, gym beam (indoor activity only)
Level of Set-up:	High

Command Task:

Set up as illustrated, with height of beam and distances adjusted to suit the group. The team must move themselves from the start point to the finish, taking the equipment with them, as quickly as possible. They are not allowed to touch the ground in between Mat A and Mat B.

Progressions:

● Introduce a burden.

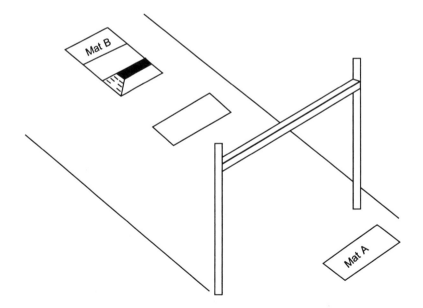

Equipment set-up

Name:	WRIST LINK
Group Size:	1–8, in pairs
Level of Activity:	Passive
Equipment:	Two skipping ropes per pair
Level of Set-up:	Low

Command Task:

Each person ties the rope ends to their wrists, first linking their rope with that of their pair. They must unlink themselves without untying the knot or slipping their wrists out.

Progressions:

- None.

Name:	DISTANT VOICES
Group size:	1–8
Level of Activity:	Active
Equipment:	One hoop per team, bags containing six items, and a list of three items from the six
Level of Set-up:	High

Command Task:

Without any form of verbal communication the control group must indicate to the receiving group which three of the six items must be placed into the bag and then the bag put into the hoop.

Note: The distance between the groups should be wide enough to stop any verbal communication. There should be equal numbers in the control group and receiving group if possible.

Progressions:

• None.

Name:	BRIDGE THAT GAP
Group Size:	1–8
Level of Activity:	Active
Equipment:	1 x 2m plank, 1 x 2.6m plank, 1 x 1.3m plank, two school benches, an easy-to-handle object
Level of Set-up:	Medium

Command Task:

With the group standing on one bench place the object within the vicinity of the furthest bench. The aim is to recover the object safely from across the gaps using only the planks, without any planks or people touching the ground. All the equipment (except the benches) to be brought back as well as the object.

Progressions:

- Introduce a burden.

Name:	HOME SWEET HOME
Group Size:	1–8
Level of Activity:	Passive
Equipment:	Paved area/as for chess, any object (eg ball) as a burden
Level of Set-up:	Low

Command Task:
The object must be transported from its start position to the home position. Players must only move in numerical order, using the Knight's move. **The burden must not touch the ground.** In order to move it may only be passed along a continuous straight or diagonal line of three people. The player holding the burden may not move.

Progressions:
- None.

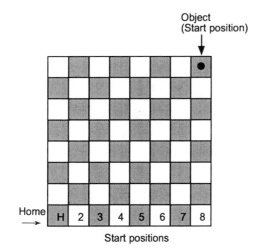

Set-up

LEVEL 4 – VERY HARD

TEAM WORKS

Name:	TEAM TRANSPORT
Group Size:	1–8
Level of Activity:	Active
Equipment:	Three oil drums or barrels, 1 x 4m plank
Level of Set-up:	Medium

Command Task:

Using the equipment provided the team must move from start to finish as quickly as possible without touching the ground. If anyone touches the ground the team must start again.

Progressions:

• Introduce a burden.

Name:	TALL ORDER*
Group size:	1–8
Level of Activity:	Active
Equipment:	Cardboard arrows, Blu-Tack, gym mats/crash mats, flat walls
Level of Set-up:	Low

Command Task:
The team must work together safely to see how high they can put the arrow up the wall.

Progressions:
- Enlarge the groups – but remember, **safety must be the first priority**.
- Establish a school record.

*Safety considerations at all times.

Name:	STAR TEAM
Group size:	7 exactly
Level of Activity:	Passive
Equipment:	Area marked on a playground with chalk, or a field with mine tape
Level of Set-up:	Low

Command Task:
Number each team member, and in turn, they must select a point to walk along a straight line to an 'open' (ie empty) point. Each successive person must start on an *empty* point and walk in a straight line to an 'open' point. Continue until there is only one 'open' point left.

Progressions:
• Introduce a burden.

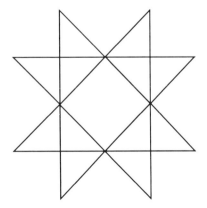

Solution: Each person must start on a point which enables them to walk to the point vacated by the previous person.

Name:	SPIDER'S WEB
Group Size:	1–8
Level of Activity:	Active
Equipment:	Spider's web (of hoops or ropes), uprights, mats
Level of Set-up:	High

Command Task:
Set up as illustrated. **Note**: the hoops must be securely tied to each other and the uprights. Pupils must work as a team to get everyone from the start to the finish by going through the spider's web. Once one person has gone through a hole then that hole cannot be used again. The spider's web must not be touched. (It might be necessary to allow team members through more than one hole. This will depend on how many 'gaps' there are and how many pupils are in a team.)

Progressions:
- Allocation of points – deduct a point for every touch.
- Adjust the height of the web.
- At low level introduce a burden: blindfolded pupil; a bench; a bucket of water; a long rope.

Name:	SIT ON IT
Group size:	16+
Level of activity:	Active
Equipment:	None

Command Task:
They must create an unsupported circle in which everyone is sitting on each other's laps. The position must be held for one minute.

Progressions:
Note: This is a fun activity for large groups on those wet days. Try achieving a year group record – a school record – a district record by challenging other schools.

• Beat the world record (about 14,000 people) – a good fund raiser!

Sit On It

Name:	ACROSS THE RAVINE
Group Size:	1–8
Level of Activity:	Very active
Equipment:	Long rope, two gym mats, three weighty objects with handles, three rounders poles, gym beam (indoors only), two short ropes, Karabiner (if possible – not necessary)
Level of Set-up:	High

Command Task:

As a team get the three objects from mat 1 to mat 2 without touching the ground in between.

Progressions:

- Introduce a burden.

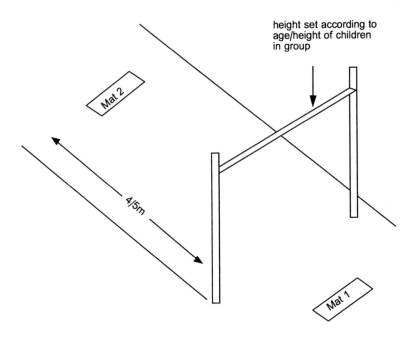

height set according to
age/height of children
in group

Mat 2

4/5m

Mat 1

Equipment set-up

Name:	TEAM TAKEOVER
Group Size:	1–8
Level of Activity:	Very active
Equipment:	The lightest gym bench, long rope, two gym mats, gym beam (indoors only)
Level of Set-up:	High

Command Task:

Set up as illustrated. The team must move from Mat 1 to Mat 2 taking their equipment with them and without them or it touching the ground.

Progressions:

- None.

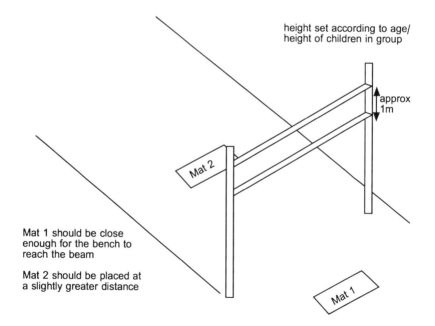

height set according to age/ height of children in group

approx 1m

Mat 2

Mat 1 should be close enough for the bench to reach the beam

Mat 2 should be placed at a slightly greater distance

Mat 1

Equipment set-up

Name:	COLOURED SQUARE
Group Size:	16+
Level of Activity:	Active
Equipment:	16 bibs/bands (eg 4 red, 3 blue, 3 green, 3 white, 3 yellow)
Level of Set-up:	Low

Command Task:
Give each person a coloured band. They must arrange themselves into a grid of 4 x 4 in which nobody is wearing the same colour in the same row, either horizontally, vertically or diagonally.

Progressions:
● There aren't any – it's bad enough as it is!

Note: This task can be used as a completion task to an assault course against the clock. In this case the solution can be provided at the outset – before the timed course in a calm and formal manner. When the teams come to perform it under the stress of 'against the clock' and being 'puffed-out', the solution will be forgotten, panic will set in and team dynamics will prove interesting.

Green	Red	White	Yellow
Yellow	Blue	Green	Red
Red	White	Yellow	Blue
Blue	Green	Red	White

Solution: to place the 'reds' first, followed by the four centre squares of other colours – the rest is easy!

97

Name:	DO IT NOW
Group Size:	Solo
Time Duration:	Six weeks
Level of Activity:	High
Equipment:	As listed

Command Task:
Results not excuses!

Progressions:
- Repeat with ease.
- Repeat and create with ease.

ENJOY THE ADVENTURE!

Bibliography

Roland, C and Havens, M (1983), *An Introduction to Adventure – A sequential approach to challenging activities with persons who are disabled*, Vinland National Center, Lorretto, Minnesota.

Pentagram (1993), *Puzzlegrams*, , Books UK Ltd: London

Belbin, R.M. (1981), *Management Teams – Why they succeed or fail*, Heinemann: London

Brandes, D. and Phillips, H. (1977), *Gamester's Handbook*, Hutchinson: London

Brooke, J. D. & Whiting, H. T. A. (1973), *Human Movement – a field study*, Henry Kimpton Publishers: London

De Bono, E. (1992), *Handbook for the Positive Revolution*, Pelican Books: London

De Bono, E. (1971), *Five Day Course in Thinking*, Pelican Books: London

DoE paper, January 1995, 'Physical Education in the National Curriculum'.

Fluegelman, A. (1978), *The New Games Book*, Sidgwick & Jackson: London

Heseltine, P. and James, P. (1983), *101 Great Games*, Carousel Books: London

Oeser, A. (1966), *Teacher, Pupil, Task*, Associated Book Publishers: London

Syer, J. (1986), *Team Spirit*, Kingswood Press: London

List of Equipment Used

A gymnasium
A paved chessboard
Balls – netball/football/tennis/medicine
Beer/milk crates
Blindfolds
Block of chalk
Cardboard and Blu-Tack
Cones – various sizes
Crash mats
Frisbees
Gym box
Gym mats
Hula hoops – large/medium/small
Karabiner
Long ropes
Map of school grounds
Mine tape
Netball posts
Oil drums/rubbish bins with fixed lid (6)
Old canoe and paddles
Old car tyres

Old towels/blankets
Planks – 4.3m, 4m, 2.6m, 2m (x2), 1.3m
Plastic bottle – 1.5 litre
Plastic downpipe – 1m length
Plastic shopping bags
Rounders poles
School dining tables
Sellotape
Skipping ropes – no handles
Skittles
Sliced wooden shapes
Team bands
Team bibs – five colours
Team skis
Telegraph pole
Tent pegs
Wall bars and beams
Wood lengths
 – 6 x (4.0m x 0.3m x 0.3m)
 – 6 x (2.6m x 1.3m x 0.3m)
 – 7 x (6.0m x 0.3m)

TASK INFORMATION SUMMARY

Cross Reference of Task Information

Task	Skills group/ indiv.	4	3	2	1	A	B	C	V	A	P	H	M	L	Page
Across the Ravine	G	•				•			•			•			94
All in Order	I		•	•		•	•			•				•	47
All Change	G			•	•	•	•			•			•		46
Blanket Ball	G		•			•			•				•		60
Blind Alley	I			•		•				•		•			58
Blind Shape	G	•				•	•	•		•				•	71
Blind Trail	I		•			•				•		•			78
Blocks, Lengths, Dowels	G	•				•				•			•		70
Bridge That Gap	G	•				•				•			•		84
Bug Tug	I			•	•	•	•		•					•	50
Catch Tail	G			•		•	•		•					•	53
Clue Orienteering	G		•			•				•			•		74
Coloured Square	G	•					•			•				•	97
Connect Four	I			•			•			•			•		56
Damsel in Distress	G			•		•	•			•				•	61
Desert Island	G		•			•				•			•		54
Distant Voices	I		•			•				•		•			83
Dry Water Paddle	I		•			•				•		•			79
Head Down Round & Round	G			•	•	•	•		•					•	48
High and Dry	G		•			•				•			•		68
Home Sweet Home	G	•				•				•				•	85
Islands	I		•			•				•				•	38
It All Adds Up	G		•				•			•				•	66
Knots	G			•	•	•				•				•	44
Mini Assault Course	I			•		•			•			•			76
People Snake	G		•				•			•		•			57
Plates of Meat	G			•	•	•				•				•	54
Pole to Pole	I			•		•				•		•			67
Raft Race	G			•		•				•			•		63
Rat Up a Drainpipe	G			•		•				•			•		62
River Crossing	G			•		•				•			•		72
Round Table	I			•		•				•				•	69
Round the Barrel	G		•				•			•				•	52
Shapes	G			•		•					•		•		75
Sit On It	G	•					•			•				•	92
Skin the Snake	G		•				•			•				•	40
Spider's Web	G	•				•				•		•			91
Star Team	G	•				•					•			•	90
Stumped	G		•			•				•				•	64
Tall Order	G	•				•				•				•	89
Team Scream	G			•		•	•	•	•					•	43
Team Ski	G		•			•				•			•		59
Team Takeover	G		•			•			•			•			96
Team Transport	G	•				•				•			•		88
Total 30	G				•		•			•				•	65
Team Transfer	G	•					•			•		•			81
26 in Line	G		•				•			•				•	80
Up and Down	G				•	•				•				•	42
Wrist Link	I		•			•				•				•	82

Key:

Skills	Task difficulty	Group size	Level of activity	Level of set-up
G – Group	1 – Easy	A – 1–8	V – Very active	H – High
I – Individual	2 – Moderate	B – 9–15	A – Active	M – Medium